Opposites

by Gillian Youldon

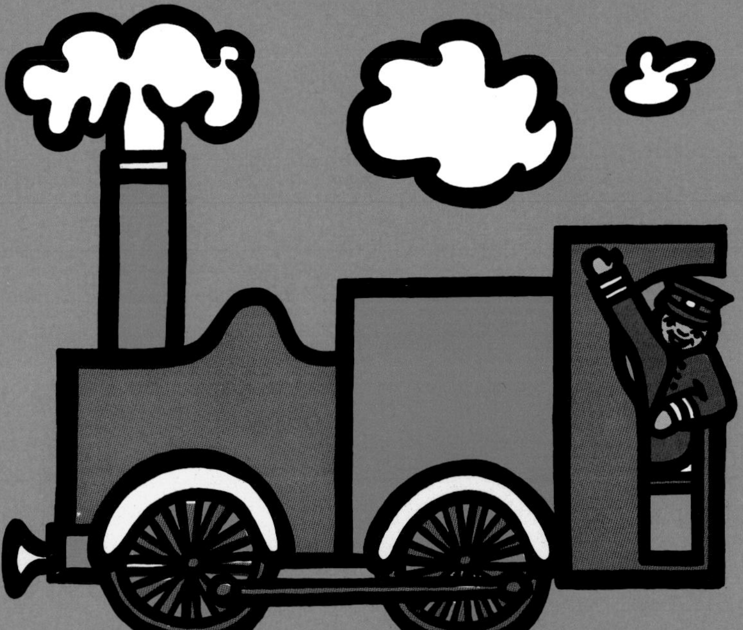

Franklin Watts · London · New York · Toronto ·

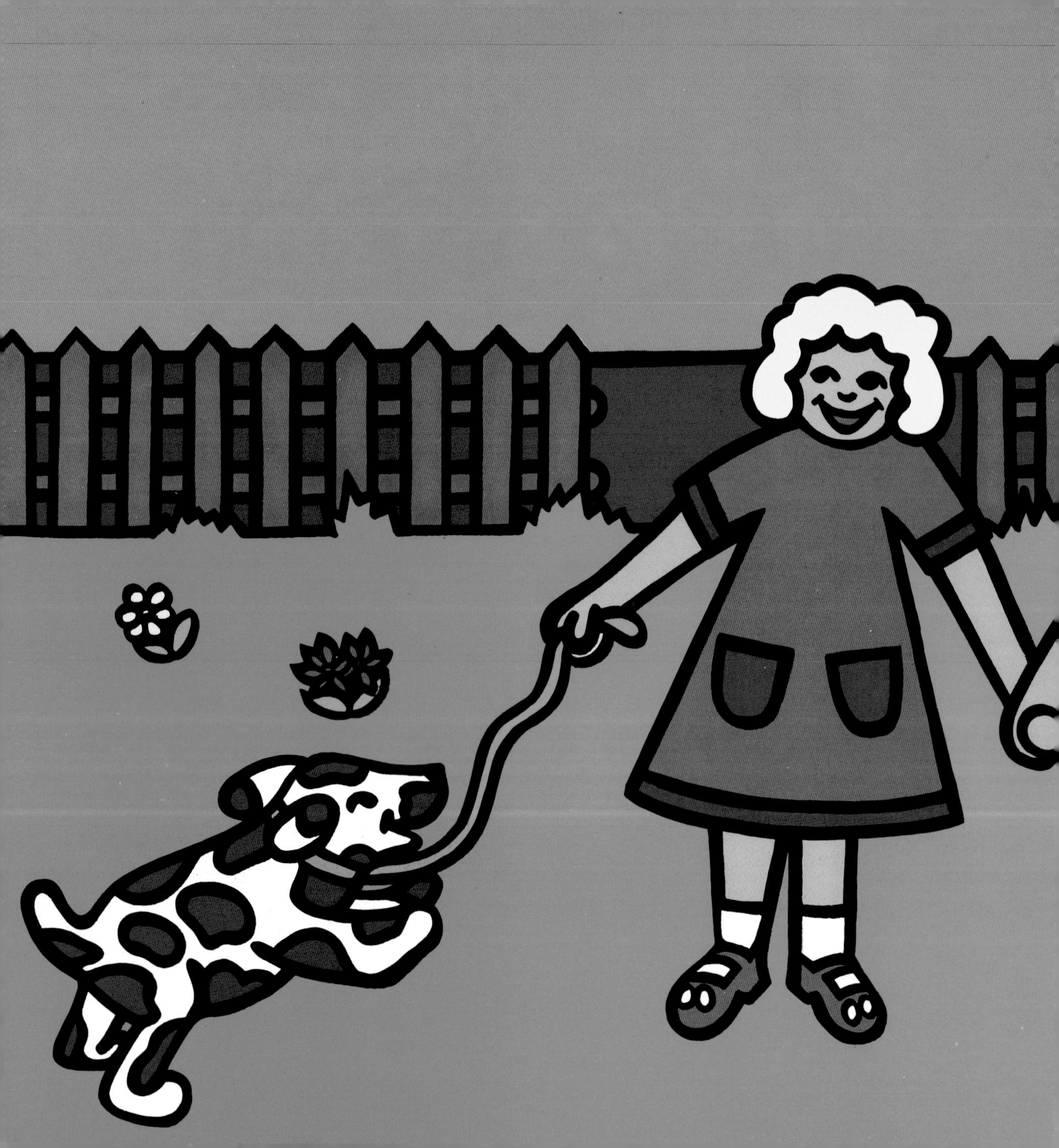

Front

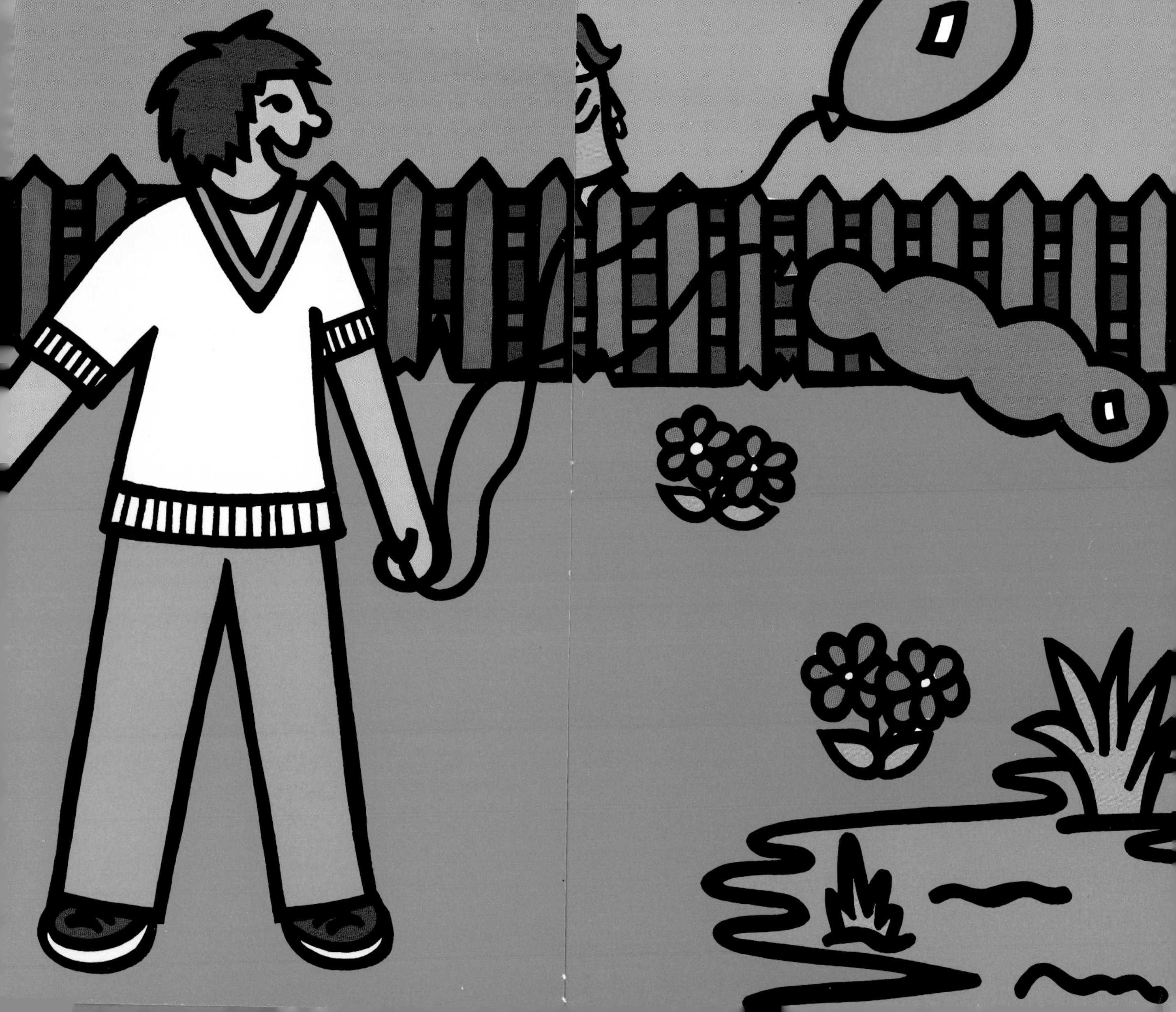

Top

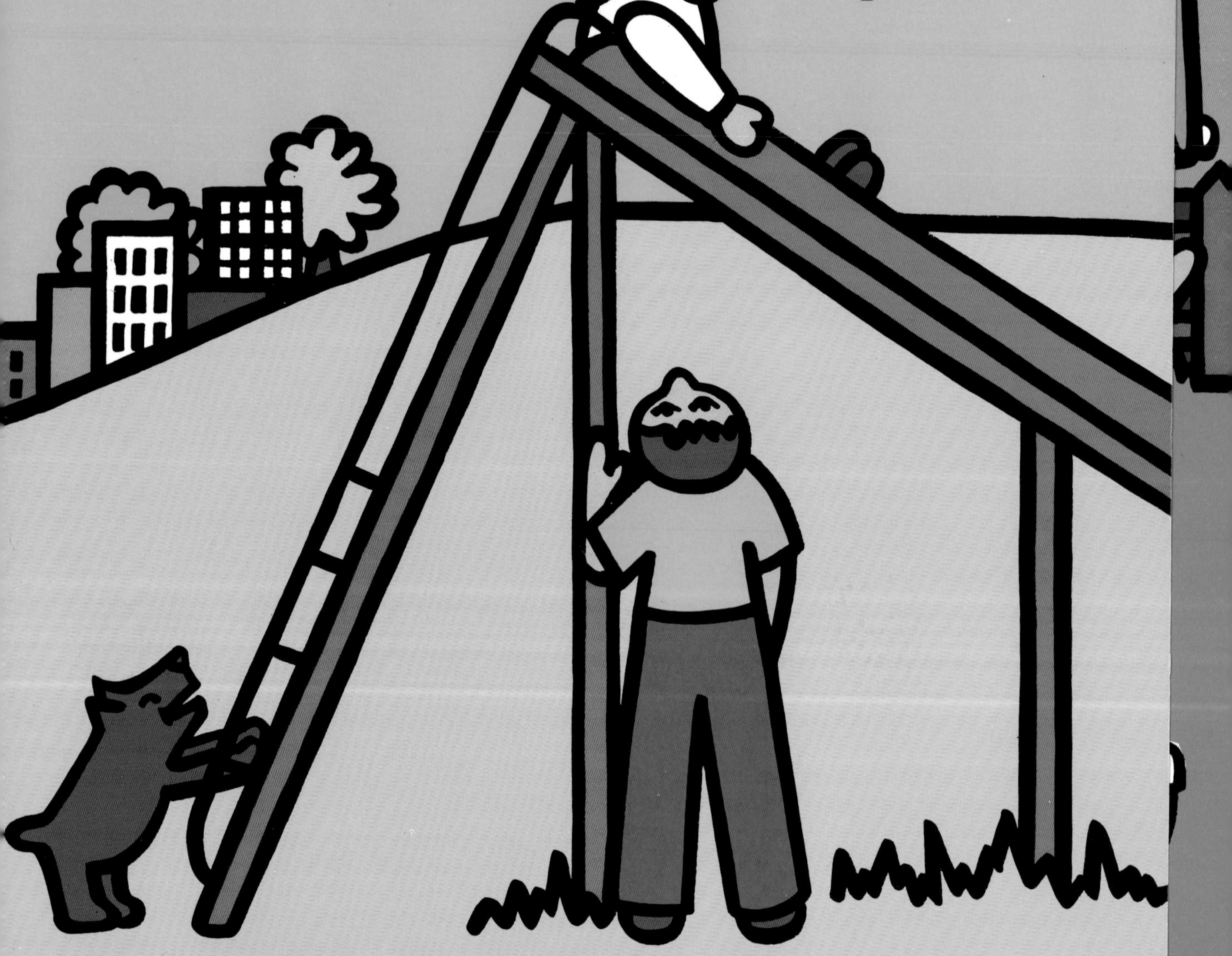

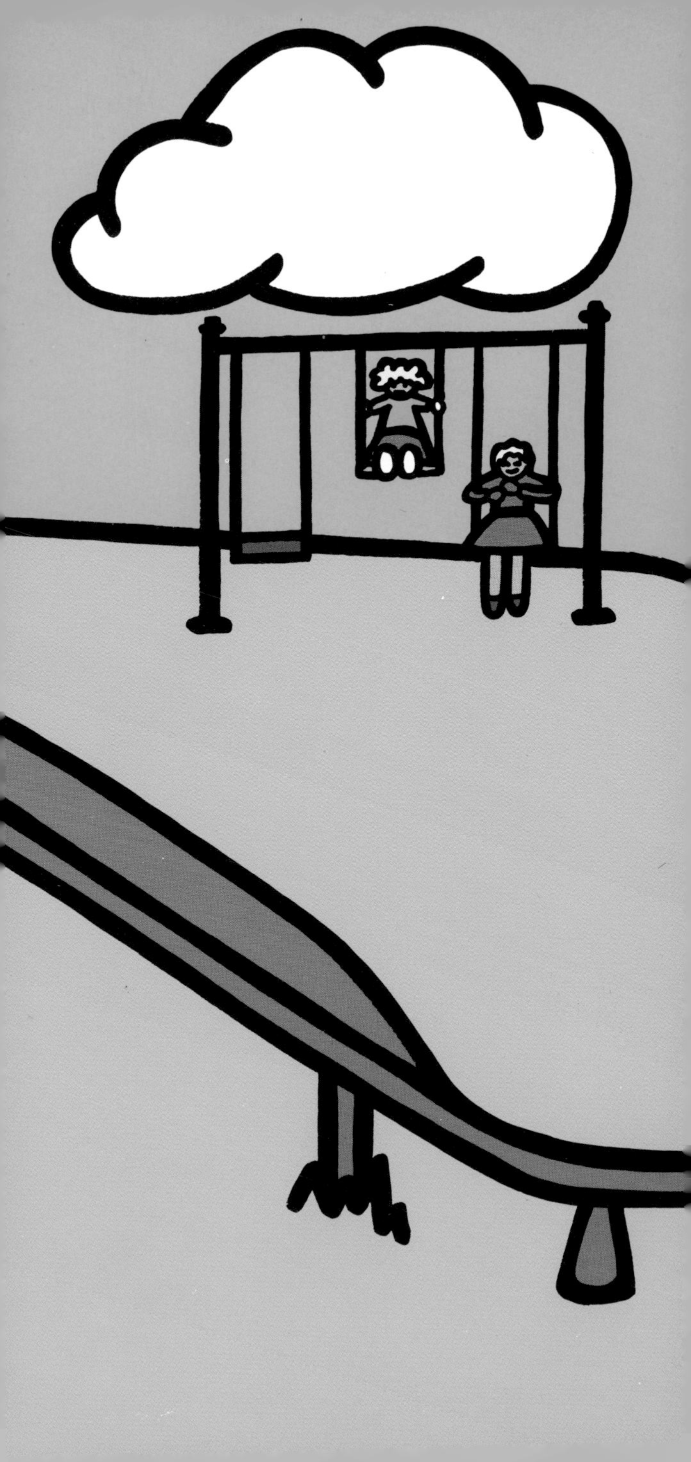

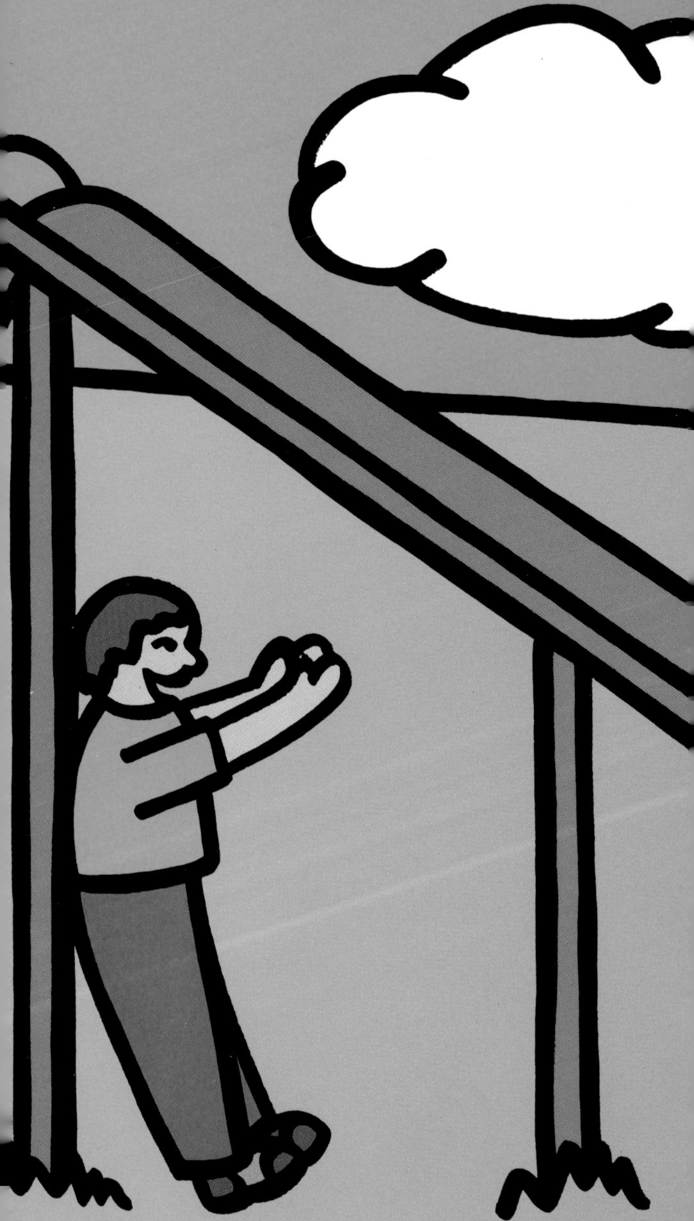

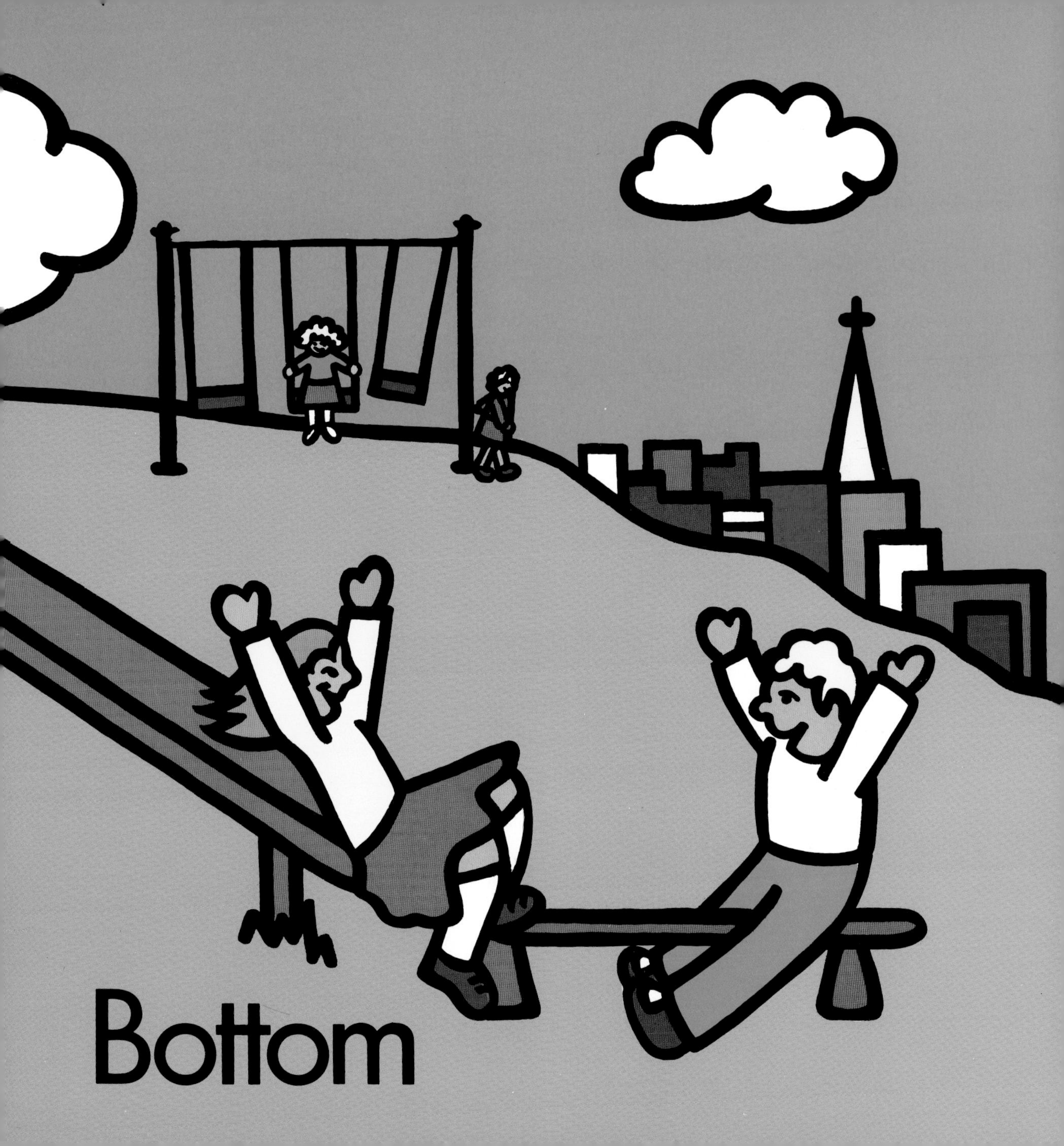

Bottom

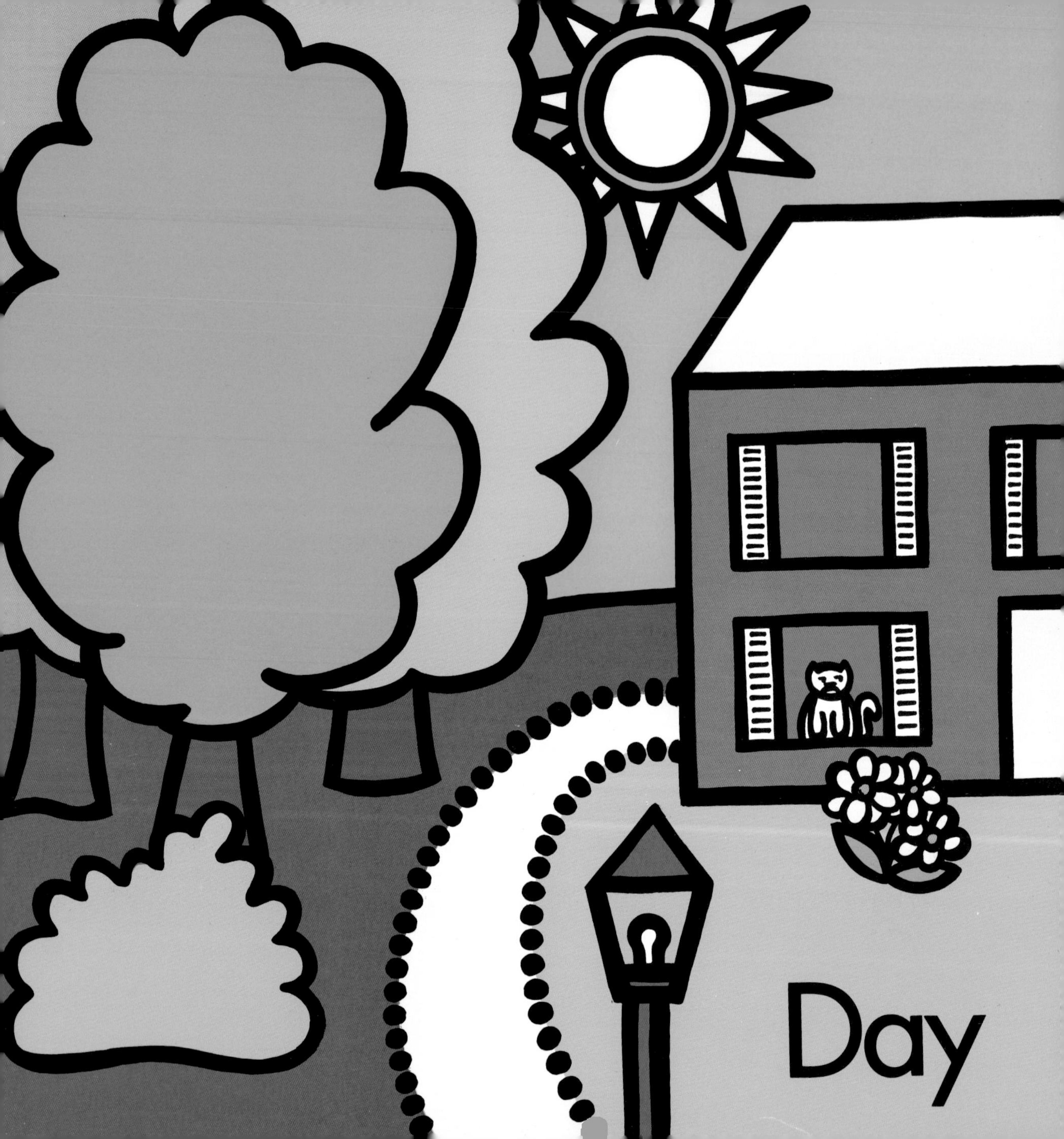
Day

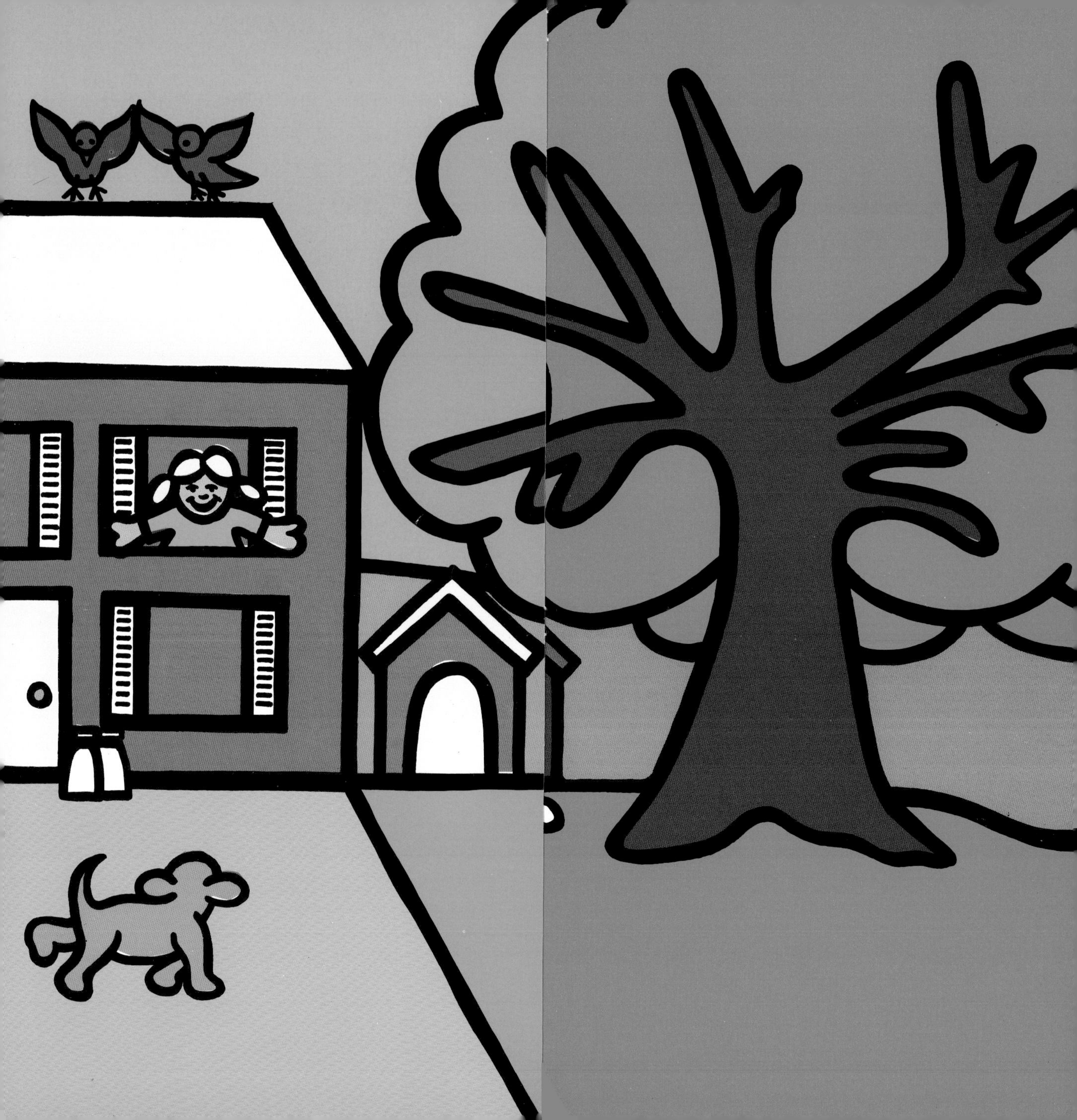

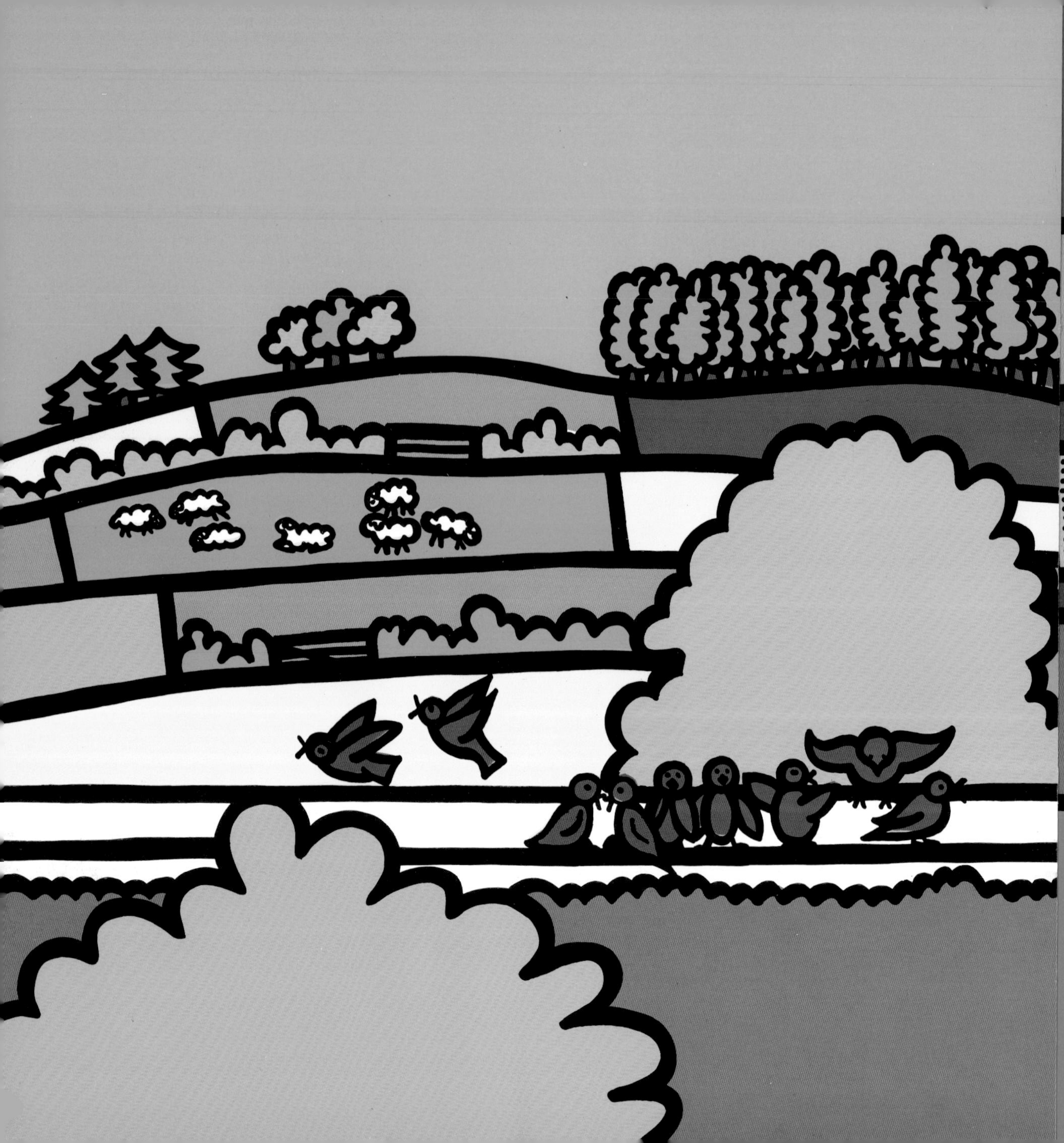

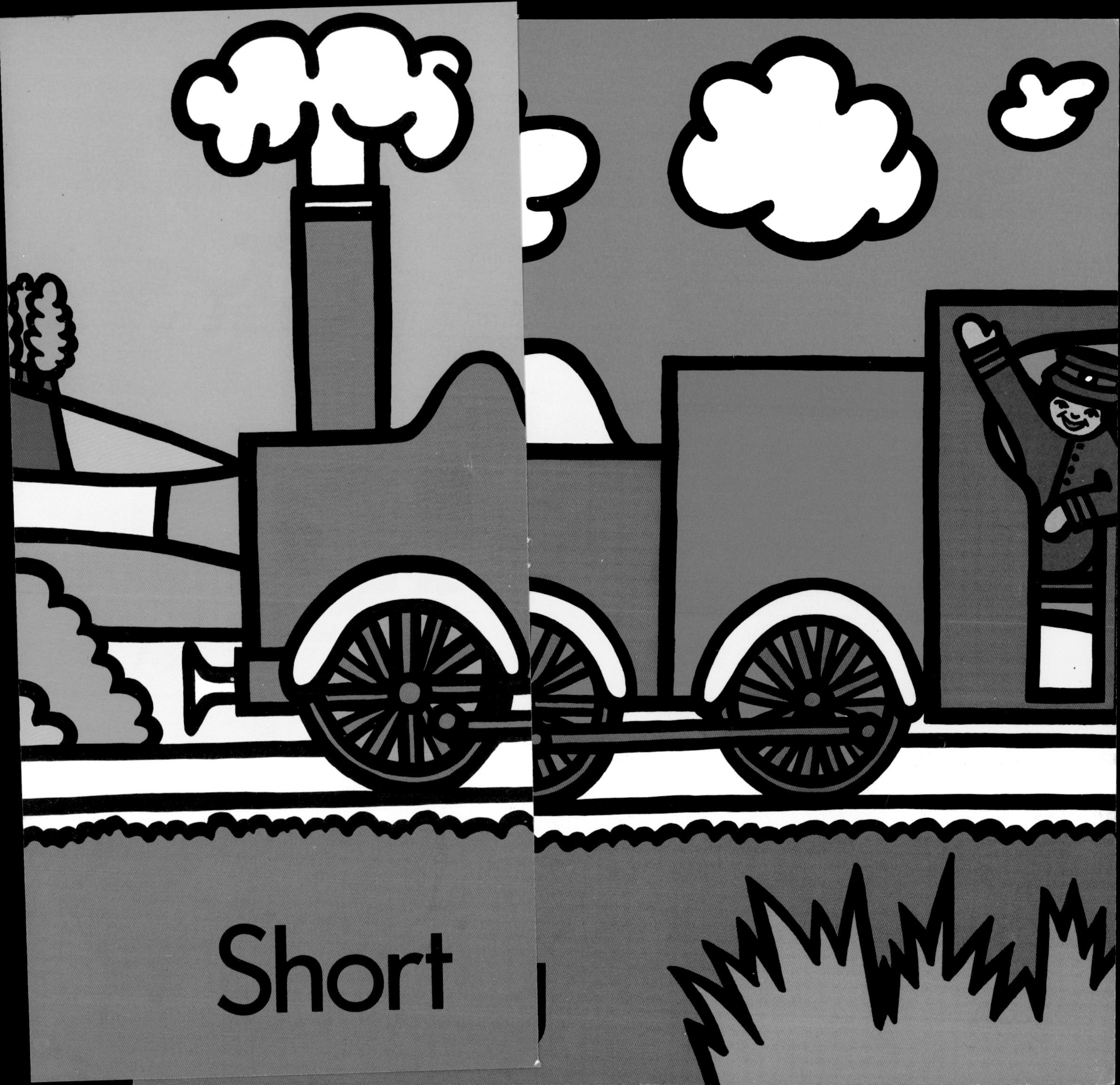

Short

Quiet

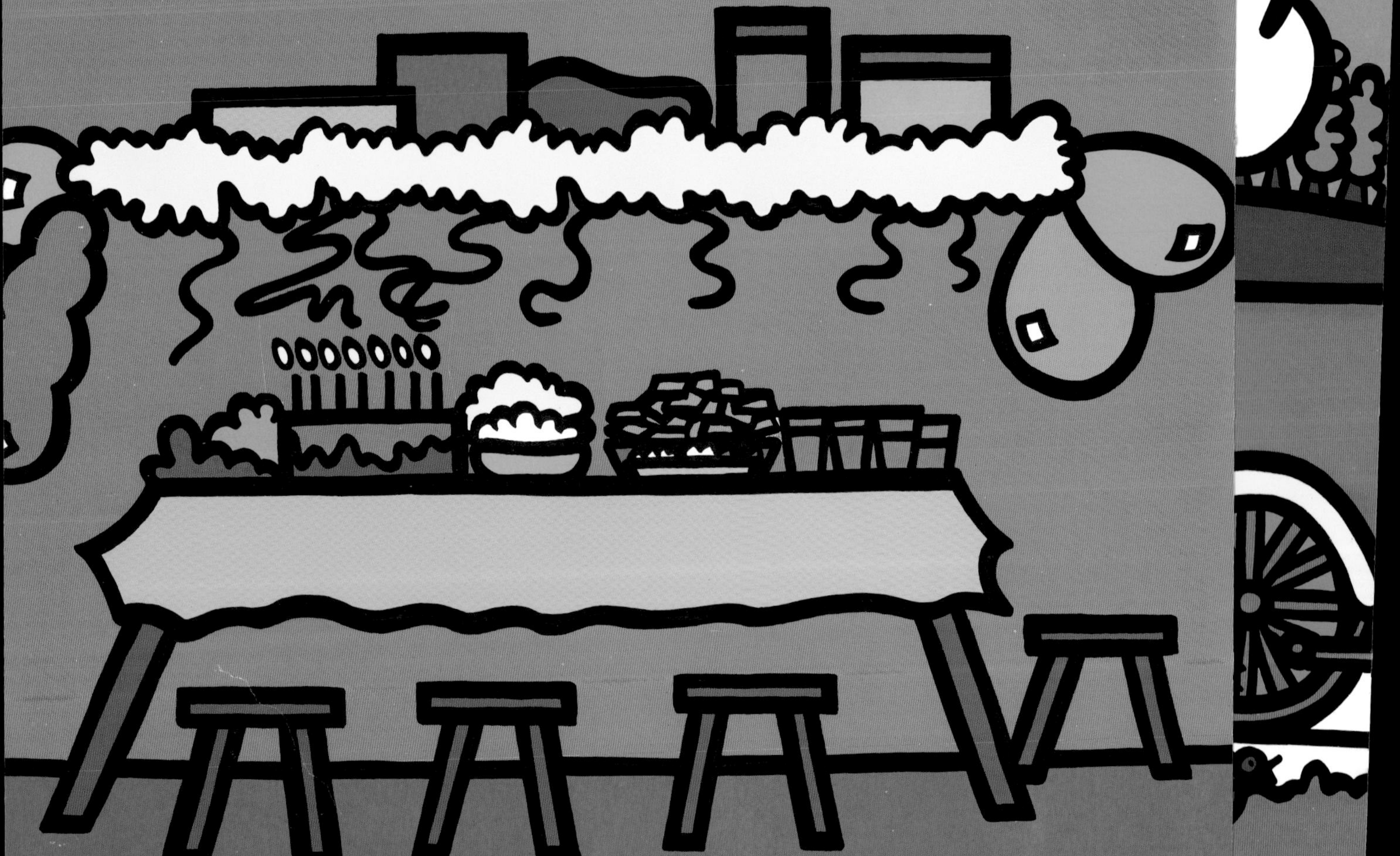

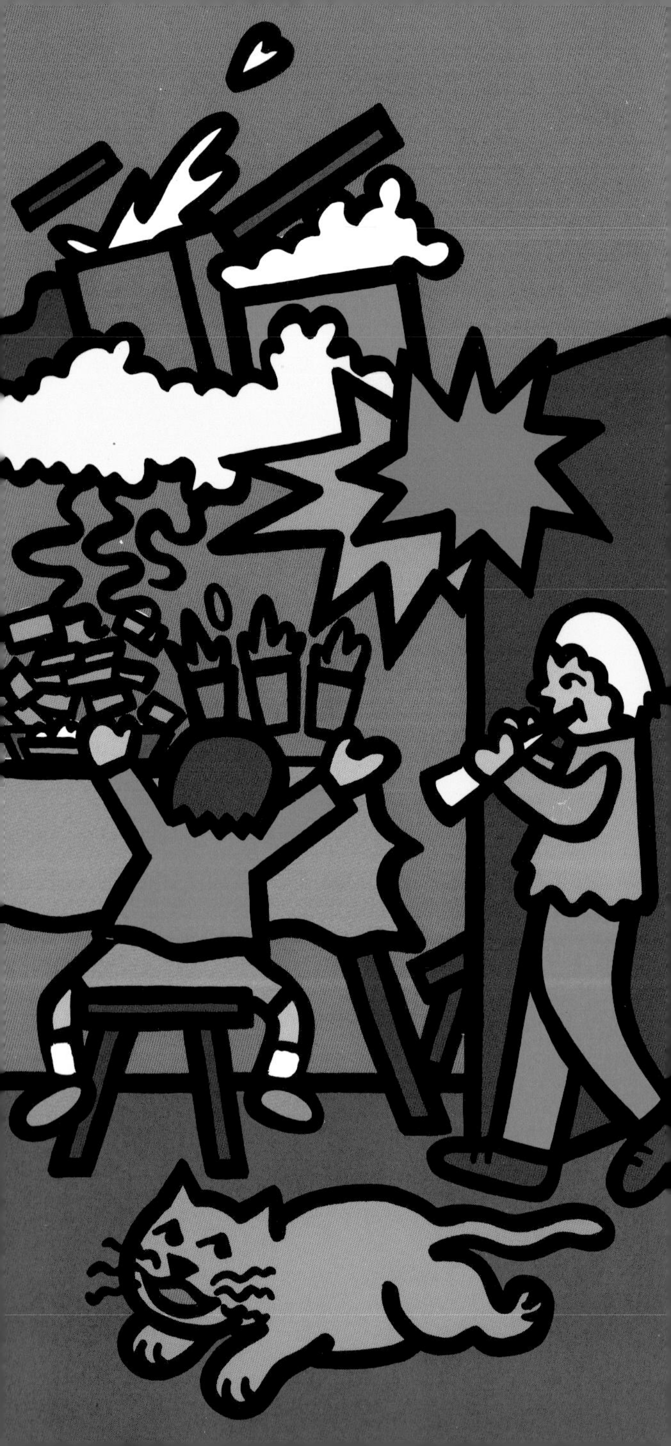

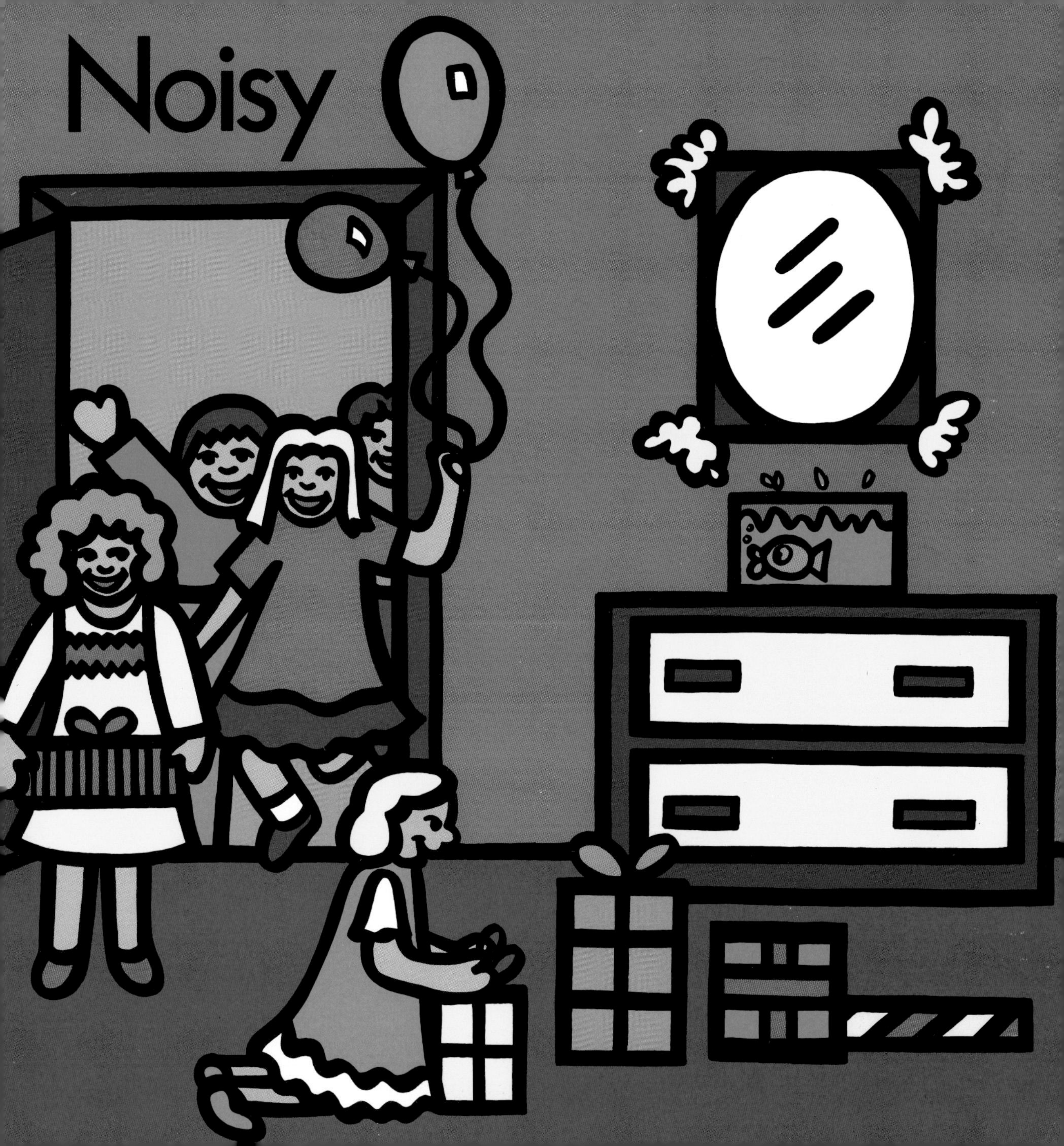
Noisy

Up

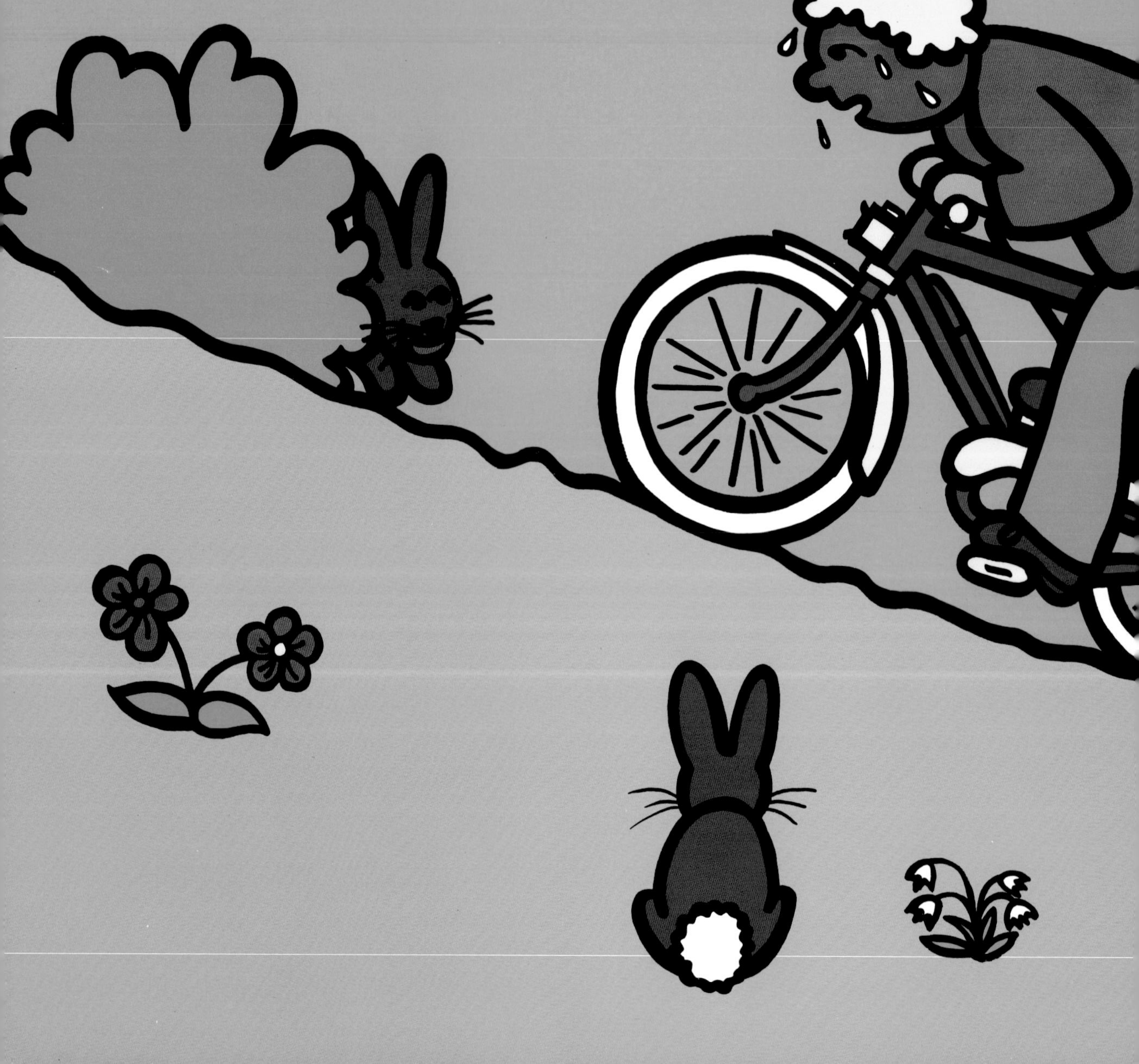

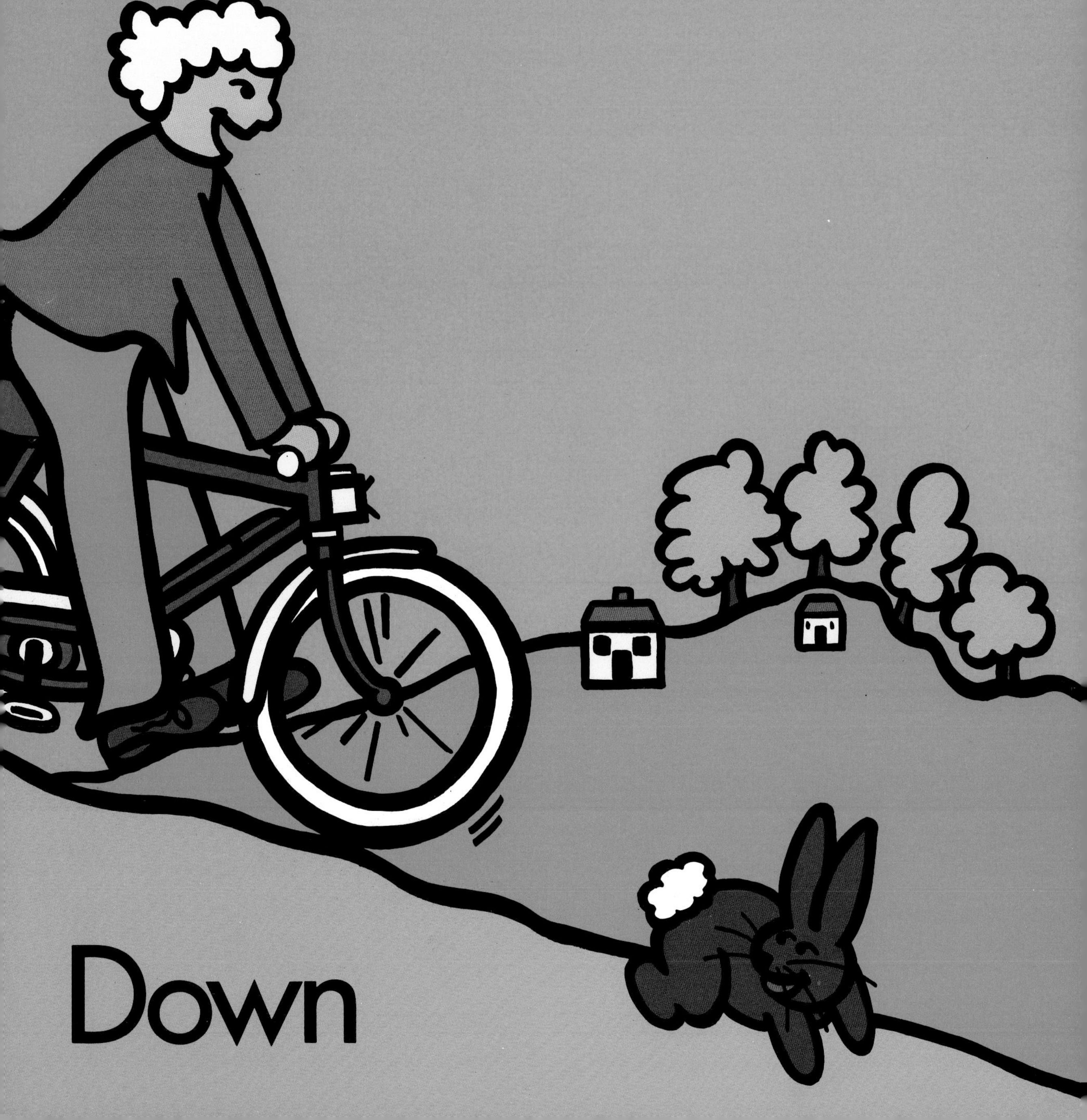

Down